FAVOURITE
CASSEROLE RI

One-pot Casseroles and Stews

SALMON

Index

Cover pictures *front:* Fireside Friends *by James Cole back:* Fireside Bliss *by L. Mortimer*
Title page: An Inn Kitchen *by Thomas Rowlandson*

Printed and Published by J. Salmon Ltd., Sevenoaks, England © Copyright

Braised Oxtail

A thick stew full of rich and succulent flavours. Use good beef dripping if possible and select a tail with plenty of meat around the bones.

1 oxtail (about 3 lbs)	4 sticks celery, chopped
2 oz beef dripping (or cooking oil)	1½ pints beef stock
2 oz seasoned flour	1 tablespoon mushroom ketchup
1 large onion, sliced	¾ teaspoon dried thyme
2-3 carrots, sliced thickly	2 bay leaves and a good sprig of parsley
1 medium turnip, roughly diced	Salt and pepper

Set oven to 300ºF or Mark 2. Remove any excess fat from the oxtail pieces, rinse and dry with kitchen paper. Toss in the seasoned flour. Melt the dripping (or heat the oil) in a large frying pan and, when really hot, fry the oxtail pieces until well browned. Transfer to a casserole dish. Next fry all the vegetables until browned around the edges, adding more dripping (or oil) if necessary, and put into the casserole with the meat. Stir the remaining seasoned flour into the pan and gradually add the stock, over the heat, stirring constantly. Add the mushroom ketchup, pour over the meat and vegetables, put in the bay leaves and parsley and season lightly. Bring to the boil on the stove then cover and simmer in the oven for about 3 hours until the meat is really tender. When cooked, remove the herbs and check the seasoning. Spoon off any excess fat from the surface before serving. Serve with creamy mashed potatoes. Serves 4.

Irish Stew

This is one of the oldest and most famous of all Irish recipes, traditionally made only with neck of lamb, potatoes and onions, flavoured with herbs.

1½ lb neck of lamb, middle or best end, cut into cutlets and trimmed
2 large onions, sliced   1 lb potatoes, peeled, sliced and weighed after preparation
2 tablespoons fresh chopped parsley and 1 teaspoon fresh chopped thyme, mixed together
Salt and black pepper   ½ to ¾ pint water

Set oven to 325ºF or Mark 3. Layer the lamb, onions and potatoes in a casserole dish, sprinkling the herbs and seasoning between each of the layers and finishing with a neat layer of potatoes on top. Pour in the water, cover with a piece of buttered greaseproof paper and put on the lid. Cook for 2 to 2½ hours. The traditional accompaniments to Irish Stew are either pickled red cabbage and/or carrots. Serves 4.

Alternatively, if desired, Irish Stew can be cooked slowly on top of the stove.

Minced Beef Casserole

This dish is best made the day before it is required, to improve the flavour.

2 lb lean minced beef	2 large onions, sliced
3 tablespoons seasoned flour	4 oz swede or turnip, cubed
3 tablespoons cooking oil	2 pints beef stock
2 oz mushrooms, sliced	1 small can tomatoes
4 carrots, cubed	Pinch of dried mixed herbs
2 sticks celery, sliced	Salt and pepper

2 teaspoons brown sugar

Set oven to 300ºF or Mark 2. Heat the oil in a large frying pan. Mix the meat with the seasoned flour and brown well in the pan. Remove to a deep casserole dish. Put the fresh vegetables in the frying pan, cover and sweat for a few minutes; then add the rest of the ingredients and mix well. Check the seasoning. Pour over the meat in the casserole and stir well. Cover and cook slowly for about 1½ hours. Serve with French fried potatoes and a green vegetable. Serves 6 to 8.

Pheasant Casserole

A brace of pheasant casseroled with red wine and brandy.

A brace of pheasant,
 prepared for cooking
A walnut of butter
4 rashers back bacon, chopped
1 tablespoon flour
Salt and black pepper
³/₄ pint chicken stock

2 onions, chopped
1 carrot, sliced
 4-6 small shallots, peeled and left whole
Bouquet garni of bayleaf, parsley and thyme
¹/₂ pint red wine
2 tablespoons brandy
6 oz button mushrooms

Set oven to 325°F or Mark 3. Melt the butter in a frying pan and quickly brown the pheasants on all sides. Remove from the pan and place in a casserole dish. Fry the bacon lightly in the residual butter, then stir in the flour and seasoning. Pour in the stock, stirring all the time. Add the onions, carrot and shallots and bring the mixture to the boil. Pour over the pheasant and add the *bouquet garni* of herbs. Pour the wine into the casserole, cover and cook for 2¹/₂ to 3 hours. Remove the herbs, add the brandy and mushrooms and cook for a further 30 minutes. Serve with creamed potatoes and a green vegetable. Serves 4.

Mustard Rabbit

Rabbit meat and pork cooked together with a rich and creamy mustard sauce.

1 young rabbit, cleaned and jointed   2 oz flour   Salt and black pepper
1 teaspoon dry mustard powder   A little cooking oil
^{1}/$_2$ lb belly pork, skinned, boned and cubed   2 carrots, sliced   1 large onion, chopped
1 tablespoon chopped fresh parsley   2 teaspoons chopped fresh thyme
1 bay leaf   Salt and black pepper ^{1}/$_2$ pint dry cider
Chicken stock   3 egg yolks   A good ^{1}/$_4$ pint double cream
1 level tablespoon dry mustard powder   Chopped fresh parsley for garnish

Set oven to 350°F or Mark 4. Mix together the flour, seasoning and mustard powder and coat the rabbit pieces. Heat the oil in a frying pan and lightly fry the rabbit joints. Place half the pork and half the vegetables in a casserole dish and place the rabbit joints on top. Add the herbs and seasoning and top with the remaining pork and vegetables. Pour the cider into a pan and bring to the boil. Pour into the casserole with sufficient hot stock just to cover. Cover and cook for 1^1/$_2$ to 2 hours until tender. Remove the meat and vegetables and place in a warm serving dish. Strain the liquid into a pan and boil to reduce. Beat together the egg yolks, cream and mustard powder, add 3 to 4 tablespoons of the liquid and whisk. Pour into the remainder of the liquid and heat through thoroughly, but do not boil or the sauce will curdle. Adjust the seasoning, adding more mustard if necessary, then spoon over the rabbit. Serve, garnished with parsley, with creamed potatoes and a green vegetable. Serves 4 to 6.

"Hearth and Home" by John Fullwood RBA

Pork Hot-Pot

A quickly made hot-pot using chicken soup and covered with potato and grated cheese.

1½ lb lean pork, cubed	1 can condensed chicken soup
2 tablespoons cooking oil	1 small can peeled tomatoes
2 medium onions, sliced	6 medium potatoes, peeled and sliced
3 oz Cheddar cheese, grated	

Set oven to 350°F or Mark 4. Remove any bones from the meat and cut into chunky cubes. Heat the oil in a frying pan and fry the onion until soft, mix in the meat cubes and brown them quickly on all sides. Transfer to a casserole dish. Add the soup and tomatoes and season to taste. Cover with the sliced potatoes and sprinkle the grated cheese over the top. Cover and cook in the oven for 2 to 2½ hours. Remove the lid for the last 20 minutes. Serve with a green vegetable. Serves 6.

Fish Casserole

Monk fish, used in this recipe, has a flavour not unlike lobster but any firm, white-fleshed fish could be substituted. In which case try adding a teaspoon of anchovy essence.

1½ pints dry cider	1 oz flour
1 oz butter	1 tablespoon fresh parsley,
1 large onion, diced	finely chopped
4 oz button mushrooms	1 teaspoon marjoram, finely chopped
1½ lb monk fish, skinned	Salt and pepper
and cut into cubes	2 tablespoons single cream

Set oven to 325ºF or Mark 3. Boil the cider rapidly in a saucepan to reduce it to 1 pint. In a separate pan melt the butter, add the onion and cook for 3 minutes. Add the mushrooms and fish and cook for 1 minute, then add the flour and stir well. Pour the cider over, stir well and add the herbs; season to taste. Transfer to a casserole dish, cover and cook for 30 minutes (or continue to cook gently on the top of the stove for 30 minutes). Stir in the cream just before serving. Serve with fresh vegetables and crusty bread. Serves 4 to 6.

Beef in Stout

A stew that dates from the 19th century, when it was often made with porter, a dark brown ale which, like stout, produces a fine, dark gravy.

2 lb stewing steak, cubed	**Salt and black pepper**
1 tablespoon oil	**2 carrots, sliced**
A walnut of butter	**$^1/_2$ pint stout**
2 onions, sliced	**1 teaspoon soft brown sugar**
2 tablespoons flour	**Chopped fresh parsley for garnish**

Heat the oil and butter in a large saucepan and cook the meat until lightly browned. Remove and set aside. Add the onions and fry until softened. Stir in the flour and seasoning, then return the meat to the saucepan with the carrots, stout and sugar. Stir well and bring to the boil, then cover and simmer gently for 2 to $2^1/_2$ hours or until the meat is tender. Serve garnished with chopped parsley and accompanied by mashed potatoes and a green vegetable. Serves 4 to 6.

If desired, a half-and-half mix of Guinness and water can be used for the gravy and a few sliced mushrooms added to the stew. Alternatively, this dish can be cooked in the oven at 350ºF or Mark 4 for the same length of time.

Celebration Lamb

A lamb and asparagus dish for special occasions.

2 lb leg of lamb, cut into 2 inch pieces	**Pinch of rosemary**
2 oz seasoned flour	**2 lb asparagus, cooked**
2 oz butter	**5 fl oz double cream**
2 onions, thinly sliced	**A few drops of fresh lemon juice**
½ pint lamb stock	**Salt and pepper**

Set oven to 325ºF or Mark 3. Melt the butter in a frying pan. Toss the meat in the seasoned flour and cook, a little at a time, in the butter until browned all over. Place in a flameproof casserole dish. Add the onions to the pan and cook for a few minutes. Add the stock with the remaining flour, stirring and, when hot, pour over the meat and mix well. Add the rosemary, cover and cook in the oven for about 1 hour until the meat is tender. Drain the meat and put on to a warm serving dish. Drain the cooked asparagus, cut off the tips and arrange them around the meat. Place the stems of the asparagus with 2 tablespoons of liquid from the casserole in a liquidizer and, when blended, return to the casserole together with the cream, lemon juice and seasoning. Re-heat on the stove, stirring all the time and then pour over the meat. Serve with baby potatoes and buttered carrots. Serves 4 to 6.

Kidney and Sausage Casserole

This is an old and economical farmhouse recipe. The flavour is improved if it is made the day before required and re-heated.

1 oz butter	2 to 3 lambs kidneys, wiped,
2 onions, sliced	cored and sliced
1 to 2 tablespoons flour, seasoned	Bouquet garni of parsley, thyme and sage
with a pinch of dry mustard powder	Salt and black pepper
1 lb pork sausages	1 to 2 pints pork stock

Chopped fresh parsley for garnish

Set oven to 300°F or Mark 2. Melt the butter in a frying pan and lightly fry the onion until soft, but still transparent, then stir in the seasoned flour. Prick the sausages lightly with a fork and place in a casserole dish with the kidneys. Add the *bouquet garni* of herbs and season. Pour the stock over the onion and flour mixture in the pan and bring to the boil, stirring, then pour sufficient into the casserole to cover the contents. Cover and cook for about 5 hours. Discard the herbs and allow the mixture to cool overnight. Next day, set oven to 325°F or Mark 3 and cook the casserole for 30 to 40 minutes until completely heated through, topping up the gravy if necessary. Sprinkle with chopped parsley and serve with mashed potatoes, carrots and a green vegetable. Serves 4.

Pork and Apricot Casserole

Dried apricots add a delicious flavour to the pork.

1 lb pork fillet	1 clove garlic, finely chopped
1-2 oz seasoned flour	1 tablespoon tomato purée
2 tablespoons cooking oil	¾ pint vegetable stock
8 button onions or shallots, chopped	3 oz dried apricots
4 oz mushrooms, sliced	1 teaspoon dried mixed herbs

Salt and pepper

Set oven to 325°F or Mark 3. Thickly slice the pork and toss in the seasoned flour. Heat the oil in a large, flameproof casserole and fry the onions and mushrooms until they are golden. Add the pork and chopped garlic and fry for a few moments, then lower the heat, add the tomato purée, stock and any remaining flour and stir. Add the apricots and mixed herbs and season well. Stir again, bring to the boil, cover, put in the oven and cook for 1½ hours or until the meat is tender. Serve with mashed potatoes, boiled rice or couscous. Serves 4.

"Fireside Glow" by Guy Lipscombe

Spicy Turkey Stew

This tasty dish is simple to prepare; just one saucepan is required.

4-6 turkey breasts, cut into slices	2 tablespoons mango chutney
1 tablespoon butter	2 tablespoons tomato purée
1 tablespoon cooking oil	2 tablespoons medium curry paste
2 medium onions, chopped	Water
3 cloves garlic, crushed	Salt

Crush the garlic with a good pinch of salt. Heat the butter and oil in a large saucepan and fry the onions gently until soft but not brown. Add the garlic. Remove from the heat, put the slices of turkey breasts in the pan, add the chutney, tomato purée and curry paste and stir well. Slowly pour on enough water to cover all the ingredients and check the salt. Bring to the boil, cover, lower the heat and simmer for 40 to 45 minutes until the turkey is tender, stirring occasionally to prevent sticking. Add more boiling water if necessary. Serve with a green salad and crusty bread. Serves 4 to 6.

Martinmas Beef

St. Martin's Day, 11th November was, by old tradition, a time of celebration in the farming community, when a spicy beef stew was eaten.

3 lb brisket of beef	**$^1/_4$ teaspoon ground cloves**
$^1/_2$ onion, sliced	**Salt**
A 1-inch piece of root ginger,	**$^1/_2$ pint white wine**
finely chopped	**2 tablespoons white wine vinegar**
3 blades mace	**1 oz cornflour, mixed to a**
$^1/_2$ teaspoon ground nutmeg	**smooth paste with a little water**

Set oven to 275°F or Mark 1. Place the beef in a casserole dish, with the onion, spices and salt to taste. Mix the wine and vinegar together and pour over. Cover, put in the oven and cook for 3 to $3^1/_2$ hours. When the meat is cooked and tender, remove and place on a warm plate. Strain the liquid into a saucepan, thicken the gravy with the cornflour which has been mixed to a smooth paste with a little water, bring to the boil and boil, stirring continually, until thickened. Serve with carrots and mashed potatoes, with the sauce served separately. Serves 4 to 6.

Chicken Hot-Pot

An all-in-one farmhouse dish with new potatoes included.

4 large chicken joints	**4 sticks celery, sliced**
1 oz seasoned flour	**4 oz button mushrooms**
2 oz butter	**Salt and black pepper**
1½ lb scraped small new potatoes	**1 pint chicken stock**
1 clove garlic, crushed	**1 heaped teaspoon dried mixed herbs**
12 baby onions, peeled	**1 teaspoon paprika pepper**
4 rashers streaky bacon, diced	**1 bayleaf**

Chopped fresh parsley for garnish

Set oven to 350ºF or Mark 4. Toss the chicken joints in the seasoned flour. Melt the butter in a frying pan and brown the chicken joints until golden all over. Place the joints in a large casserole dish and add the potatoes. Put the garlic, onions, bacon, celery and mushrooms in the pan and cook for a few minutes. Add the remaining flour and stir in well. Add the stock gradually, stirring constantly. Add the herbs and paprika and check the seasoning. Pour over the chicken and potatoes. Add the bayleaf, cover and cook for about 1 to 1¼ hours until the meat is tender. Remove the bayleaf and garnish with parsley. Serve with carrots. Serves 4.

Monmouth Stew

In Wales, lamb has always been a popular ingredient for stews and casseroles and this Welsh recipe contains leeks and pearl barley.

1½ lb stewing lamb, cubed or	2 oz pearl barley
8 lamb chops, trimmed	4 sprigs of parsley, 1 sprig of thyme
1 oz seasoned flour	and a bayleaf, tied together with string
1 oz butter or oil	Salt and black pepper
4 to 6 leeks, cut into rings	¾ to 1 pint lamb stock

Set oven to 350ºF or Mark 4. Toss the lamb in the seasoned flour. Heat the butter or oil in a frying pan and lightly fry the meat all over for 1 minute. Add the leeks and fry for a further minute, then transfer to a casserole dish. Add the pearl barley, herbs and seasoning, then pour over the stock. Bring to the boil, cover and cook in the oven for 1½ to 2 hours. Remove the *bouquet garni* of herbs before serving and serve with boiled potatoes. Serves 4.

Alternatively, if desired, the stew can be cooked gently, covered, on top of the stove until the meat is tender.

Wild Duck with Apples

When obtainable, wild duck has a distinctive, slightly gamey flavour, but a domestic bird can be used perfectly well instead.

2 wild ducks or 1 duck approx. 4-5 lb, prepared
3 oz butter   1 tablespoon oil   3 tablespoons brandy   ¹/₄ pint white wine
¹/₂ pint chicken stock   Juice of ¹/₂ orange   Salt and pepper

APPLE SAUCE
1 lb cooking apples, peeled, cored and sliced   4 tablespoons cider or water
2-3 tablespoons sugar   2 tablespoons butter   Pinch of cinnamon (if desired)

Set oven to 325°F or Mark 3. Wipe the bird(s) inside and out, dry the skin with kitchen paper and rub the skin with salt and freshly ground pepper. Heat the butter and oil in a large flameproof casserole and brown the duck(s) all over. Warm the brandy, pour over the duck(s) and set aflame. Next, pour over the wine and stock, bring to the boil, cover and cook in the oven for 1¹/₂ to 2 hours. When cooked, transfer the duck(s) to a serving dish and keep hot. Meanwhile, strain the cooking juices into a bowl, spoon off the surface fat and return to the casserole. Add the apple sauce and orange juice, heat through and stir well. Pour over the duck(s) and serve with boiled potatoes and a green vegetable. Serves 4. **Apple sauce.** Simmer the apples in a saucepan with the cider or water until soft, add the sugar and butter and cinnamon (if desired) and beat well.

Rich Venison Casserole

The gamey flavour of the meat is complemented by the rich, piquant and creamy sauce.

2 lb venison, cubed
2 tablespoons cooking oil or dripping
4 oz smoked bacon, diced
1 large onion, roughly diced
1 oz flour
1½ pts beef stock
5 fl oz port wine

8 oz cranberries
8 oz chestnuts, whole or
** roughly chopped (tinned or fresh)**
4 oz button mushrooms
1 bayleaf
Salt and pepper
3 fl oz double cream

Set oven to 275°F or Mark 1. If using fresh chestnuts, split the skins with a knife and cook them in hot water for about 5 minutes; then, while still warm, remove the outer skins and inner membranes. Heat the oil or dripping in a flameproof casserole dish and brown the venison cubes. Add the bacon and onion and cook for 3 to 4 minutes. Stir in the flour and cook for 1 minute, then pour in the stock and port wine and add the cranberries, chestnuts, mushrooms and bayleaf. Season to taste. Bring slowly to simmering point, cover and cook in the oven for 2 to 2½ hours or until the meat is tender. Remove from the oven and stir in the cream. Serve with creamy mashed potato. Serves 4 to 6.

"A Fireside Read" by William Bromley

Pork and Pepper Stew

This tasty pork stew is filled with vegetables and flavoured with yeast extract.

2 lbs lean pork	**1 large leek, thinly sliced**
Seasoned flour	**1 red or yellow pepper, de-seeded**
Oil for frying	**and cut into strips**
1 pint vegetable stock	**8 oz mushrooms, sliced**
$\frac{1}{2}$-$1\frac{1}{2}$ teaspoons yeast extract	**2 sticks celery, medium sliced**
2 large onions, chopped	**2 teaspoons mixed dried herbs**
1 large parsnip, diced	**Salt and pepper**

Cut the meat into 1 inch cubes and toss in the seasoned flour. Put 2 tablespoons of oil in a large pan and fry the meat until browned all over. Reduce the heat and add the stock and yeast extract and stir. Bring to the boil, cover and set to simmer over a low heat. Meanwhile gently fry the onions, adding a little more oil if necessary, until soft but not brown and then add to the meat with all the other prepared vegetables and the herbs. Season well. Cover, bring back to the boil and continue simmering, keeping the mixture just covered with water, until the meat is tender, about $1\frac{1}{2}$ to 2 hours; long, slow cooking is essential. Serves 6.

Maldon Boiled Beef

A warming meal flavoured with the famous Maldon Crystal Sea Salt from Essex,
which adds an especial flavour to the meat.

2 lb piece of topside or silverside of beef	1 large leek, sliced
1 large onion, peeled	Bouquet garni of mixed herbs
2 cloves	6 Peppercorns
1 large carrot, sliced	Water
	Maldon Crystal Sea Salt

Peel the onion and stud with the cloves. Prepare the carrot and leek and place with the meat and all the other ingredients, except the salt, in a saucepan. Cover with water, bring to the boil, cover the pan and simmer until the meat is cooked and tender. Lift the meat out of the stock on to a serving dish. Serve the meat sliced, with a good grinding of Maldon Crystal Sea Salt over each slice, together with the accompanying vegetables and with boiled potatoes. The surplus stock can be reserved and used for making soup. Serves 4-6.

Jugged Hare

The name comes from the lidded stoneware jug in which this dish was originally cooked.
A normal, lidded casserole will serve equally well.

1 hare, prepared and cut into joints   Seasoned flour   1¹/₂ oz butter
1 tablespoon cooking oil   1 medium onion, peeled and stuck with cloves
1 small lemon, wiped and quartered
4 sprigs parsley, 2 sprigs thyme and 2 bayleaves, tied with string
Small blade of mace   4 peppercorns   Pinch of ground nutmeg   Salt
1 pint beef stock   2 tablespoons redcurrant jelly   4 fl oz red wine

Set oven to 350°F or Mark 4. Toss the hare joints in the seasoned flour. Melt the butter and oil together in a large frying pan and brown the joints quickly on all sides. Remove from the pan and place in a large casserole dish with the onion, lemon, herbs, spices and seasoning. Pour in the beef stock, bring to the boil, cover and cook for 3 hours. Remove the joints from the casserole, place on a serving dish and keep warm. Strain the liquid into a saucepan and bring to the boil, stir in the redcurrant jelly and red wine and reheat, but do not boil. Pour over the joints and serve with forcemeat balls and grilled bacon rolls or croûtons. Serve with jacket potatoes and a green vegetable. Serves 4 to 6.

Welsh Beef Stew

This all-in-one hot-pot would, in times past, have provided two meals; meat and vegetables for one and broth for another.

1 oz butter
1½ lb stewing steak, cubed
8 oz streaky bacon rashers,
  each cut into four
1 tablespoon flour
1½ to 2 pints water
2 onions, sliced
2 carrots, sliced

2 small turnips, cubed
1 heaped dessertspoon chopped fresh herbs
  (parsley, thyme, sage, etc. mixed)
Salt and white pepper
¼ pint cider
½ lb potatoes, weighed after peeling
3 leeks, cut into rings
Chopped fresh parsley for garnish

Melt the butter in a large saucepan and fry the beef and bacon lightly, then sprinkle over the flour and fry for a further minute. Add the water and bring to the boil, then cover and simmer for 40 minutes. Allow to cool slightly and skim, then add the onions, carrots and turnips, herbs and seasoning and bring to the boil. Add the cider, cover and simmer for 1 hour. Add the potatoes and leeks, cover and simmer for a further 20 to 30 minutes. Serve, sprinkling each portion with a little finely chopped parsley. Serves 4 to 6.

Chicken and Bacon Casserole

A whole chicken casseroled in red wine with onions, mushrooms and bacon.

4 lb oven-ready fresh chicken	**8 oz button mushrooms**
2 tablespoons cooking oil	**1 clove garlic, crushed**
2 oz butter	**1 teaspoon dried mixed herbs**
6 oz bacon, cubed	**1 bayleaf**
12 small onions, peeled	**1 pint red wine**

Salt and black pepper

Set oven to 325ºF or Mark 3. Heat the butter and oil in a large frying pan and brown the chicken all over. Remove from the pan and place in a casserole dish. Fry the bacon, onions, mushrooms and garlic for a few minutes in the residual oil, add the herbs, bayleaf, seasoning and wine and mix well. Pour over the chicken. Cover and cook for $1\frac{1}{2}$ to 2 hours until the chicken is tender. Place the chicken on a warmed serving dish and keep hot. Remove the bayleaf. Strain the liquid and thicken, if necessary, with a little cornflour mixed with a little cold water and brought to the boil and serve as gravy. Serve with boiled potatoes and brussels sprouts arranged around the chicken on the dish. Serves 6.

Sweet Mutton Stew

In the old days mutton was used for this recipe but, today, lamb serves equally well.

1½ lb neck of mutton or lamb   2 teaspoons redcurrant jelly
2 onions, chopped   3 carrots, chopped   1 turnip, diced
6 oz mushrooms, sliced   1 parsnip, blanched and chopped
1 tablespoon tomato purée   1 pint vegetable stock or water

DUMPLINGS
4 oz self raising flour   2 oz shredded suet   1 teaspoon chopped parsley

Set oven to 375°F or Mark 5. Cut the meat into 1 inch cubes and put in the bottom of a large casserole dish. Spread the meat with the redcurrant jelly and cook in the oven for 15 minutes. Remove from the oven and add the chopped vegetables and a little salt and pepper. Stir the tomato purée into the stock or water and pour over the meat and vegetables. Return to the oven. Reduce the heat to 350°F or Mark 4 and cook, covered, for about 1½ hours until the meat is tender. **Dumplings:** mix together the flour, suet, parsley and seasoning with just enough water to form a stiff dough. This should make about six small dumplings. Add the dumplings to the stew for the last 30 minutes of the cooking time. Serve with buttered mashed potatoes and a green vegetable. Serves 4 to 6.

"Fireside Warmth" by T. Noyes Lewis

Stewed Kidneys

A thick brown gravy flavoured with cooking apples makes this a succulent kidney dish.

**12 lambs kidneys, skinned, cored
  and halved**
Seasoned flour
1½ oz butter
1½ pints rich brown stock
**3 sprigs parsley, 1 sprig of thyme
  and a bayleaf, tied together with string**

2 onions, cut into rings
**2 cooking apples, peeled, cored
  and cut into thick rings**
1½ oz butter
1 level tablespoon cornflour
Salt and black pepper
Chopped fresh parsley for garnish

Set oven to 300°F or Mark 2. Toss the kidneys in the well seasoned flour. Melt the butter in a frying pan and fry the kidneys quickly on both sides to seal. Place in a casserole dish. Bring the stock to the boil and pour over the kidneys. Add the herbs, cover and place in the oven. Fry the onion and apple rings in the remaining butter for 2 to 3 minutes and add to the casserole. Lower the oven temperature to 250°F or Mark ½, cover the casserole and cook for 4 hours. Before serving, thicken the gravy with the cornflour which has been mixed to a smooth paste with a little water, remove the herbs and season lightly. Serve garnished with chopped parsley and accompanied by thick slices of hot, fresh toast. Serves 4.

Braised Beef and Mushrooms

Port wine and mushrooms add flavour to this simple casserole dish.

1 lb chuck steak cut into 2 inch pieces	2 wineglasses of port wine
1½ oz butter	½ teaspoon dried mixed herbs
½ lb small onions	1 bayleaf
1 tablespoon flour	Salt and pepper
½ pint beef stock	½ lb flat mushrooms, sliced

Set oven to 350ºF or Mark 4. Melt 1 oz of the butter in a flameproof casserole dish and brown the meat on all sides. Remove from the dish and set aside. Peel the onions, melt the remaining butter in the casserole and cook the onions for a few minutes. Stir in the flour, blend in the stock and bring to the boil, stirring continually. Return the steak to the pan and stir in the port wine, herbs, bayleaf, salt and pepper. Bring back to the boil, put the lid on the casserole and cook in the oven for 1½ hours or until the meat is tender. Slice the mushrooms and add to the casserole; cover again and cook for a further ½ hour. Serves 4.

Pigeon and Parsnips

Keeping down the pigeon population is a constant battle for farmers to protect their crops. In this recipe pigeons are converted into a tasty dish with parsnips.

4 pigeons, plucked and dressed	**2 onions, chopped**
2 small parsnips	**1 dessertspoon flour**
2 oz butter	**Salt and pepper**
4 oz unsmoked streaky bacon, chopped	**Bunch of fresh herbs**

Blanch the parsnips in boiling salted water for a few minutes. Drain, cut into slices and set aside and keep the water. In a large saucepan, sauté the pigeons in the butter until brown on all sides. Add the chopped bacon and chopped onions. Then sprinkle with the flour. Mix well and add the parsnip cooking water and the sliced parsnips. Season, add the herbs and simmer over a low heat for about $1^1/_2$ to 2 hours until tender. Serve with creamed potatoes and a green vegetable. Serves 4.

Beef Stew with Walnuts

A rich and nutty beef stew.

1 lb stewing steak, cubed	2 sprigs thyme and 4 sprigs parsley,
Seasoned flour	tied together with string
1 oz dripping	$\frac{1}{2}$ oz butter
1 onion, sliced	12 button mushrooms
2 fl oz red wine	2 oz walnuts, roughly chopped
1 pint beef stock	1 stick of celery, chopped
Salt and black pepper	A little grated orange peel for garnish

Cut the steak into 2 inch cubes and toss in a little seasoned flour. Melt the dripping in a large saucepan and fry the meat until lightly browned. Remove the meat and set aside. Fry the onion in the residual dripping until golden. Return the meat to the pan and add the wine, stock, *bouquet garni* and seasoning. Bring to the boil, then cover and simmer for $1\frac{1}{2}$ to 2 hours. Fry the mushrooms, walnuts and celery in the butter and add to the stew after 1 hour of cooking. Remove the herbs and transfer the stew to a heated serving dish. Serve garnished with grated orange peel and accompanied by creamed potatoes and a green vegetable. Serves 4.

Shearers Stew

A simple stew made with leg of lamb and brown ale.

1½ lb leg of lamb, trimmed and cut into 1 inch cubes	½ pint brown ale
3 tablespoons cooking oil	½ pint lamb stock
1 oz butter	2 carrots, sliced
2 onions, thinly sliced	Salt and pepper
1 oz flour	4 thick slices of fresh white bread, cut into triangles

Set oven to 350ºF or Mark 4. Heat the oil in a frying pan, add the butter and, when hot, brown the lamb in small batches and transfer to a casserole dish. Add the onions to the frying pan and cook gently until soft. Stir in the flour and cook for 3 to 4 minutes. Remove from the heat and stir in the brown ale and stock. Return to the heat and bring to the boil, stirring. Add the carrots and seasoning to the casserole. Pour the liquid over all, cover and cook for 1 hour. Remove from the oven and stir well. Dip the bread into the liquid and arrange attractively on top. Return to the oven, uncovered, and cook for a further 30 minutes. Serves 4 to 6.

Rich Beef Stew

This Scottish stew is thickened with oatmeal rather than flour.

1 lb stewing steak, cubed	$^1/_4$ lb mushrooms, sliced
1 tablespoon cooking oil	2 tablespoons tomato purée
1 large onion, chopped roughly	1 teaspoon redcurrant jelly
4 oz smoked bacon rashers, diced	1 pt beef stock
2 tablespoons oatmeal	5 fl oz red wine
$^1/_4$ small swede, diced	Salt and pepper

Heat the oil in a large saucepan and brown the steak on all sides; then add the onions and cook for a further 2 minutes. Add the bacon and cook for another 2 minutes. Remove from the heat, stir in the oatmeal and then add the diced swede and the mushrooms. Add the tomato purée and redcurrant jelly, pour in the stock and wine and stir well. Season, return to the heat, bring slowly to simmering point, cover and cook slowly for about $1^1/_2$ to 2 hours until the meat is tender. Check the seasoning before serving. Serves 4.

"A Highland Hearth" by H. J. Dobson RSW

Ragout of Lamb

Ragouts, or spicy stews, have been popular from the 16th century to the present day.

**1 breast of lamb   Seasoned flour   2 oz butter   1 to 1½ pints lamb stock
1 onion, peeled and left whole   15 cloves   3 carrots, finely sliced
4 sprigs parsley, 1 sprig thyme, 1 small sprig rosemary and a bayleaf tied with string
4 oz mushrooms, sliced   A walnut of butter   2 teaspoons lemon juice
Salt and black pepper   4 tablespoons cooked broad beans or peas or frozen peas
Chopped fresh parsley for garnish**

Cut the lamb into cubes, removing as much fat as possible and toss in the seasoned flour. Melt the butter in a frying pan and fry the lamb until golden. Heat the stock in a large saucepan. Stick the onion with the cloves, add to the stock and bring to the boil. Add the meat, cover and simmer for 30 minutes. Lightly brown the carrots in the residual butter and add to the meat, together with the *bouquet garni* and simmer for 1½ to 2 hours, stirring from time to time. Lightly fry the mushrooms in the walnut of butter with the lemon juice. Season and add to the meat together with the broad beans or peas. Remove the herbs and the onion and cook for a further 10 to 15 minutes. Serve, garnished with chopped parsley and with creamed potatoes. Serves 4 to 6.

Rabbit and Apple Stew

A simple way to convert rabbit joints into a tasty meal.

4-6 joints of rabbit
Seasoned flour
2 oz butter
2 medium onions, chopped
2 medium carrots, sliced
2 medium apples, peeled,
  cored and thickly sliced

8 oz mushrooms, sliced
8 oz streaky bacon, cut into 1 inch pieces
$1/2$ pint vegetable stock
2 teaspoons tomato purée
Sprig of fresh thyme or
  1 teaspoon dried thyme
Salt and pepper

Heat half the butter in a large saucepan and cook the onions, carrots and apples for 5 minutes, stirring well. Remove from the pan and set aside. Toss the rabbit joints in the seasoned flour. Heat the remaining butter in the pan and brown the rabbit joints on both sides. Lower the heat, add the mushrooms and bacon pieces and continue cooking for 5 minutes. Add the stock slowly and then add the apple/vegetable mixture, the tomato purée and thyme, stirring all the time, and season. Bring to the boil, cover, lower the heat and simmer for 1 hour or until the rabbit is tender. Stir occasionally and add more stock or boiling water if required. Serves 4 to 6.

Bacon and Beans

This is a centuries old cottager's dish which make a little go a long way.

2 to 2½ lb forehock of bacon, diced   **Black pepper**
3 to 4 onions, chopped   **Pinch of dry mustard powder**
½ lb haricot beans   **A bayleaf**
Water or pork stock

Place the haricot beans in a bowl of cold water and leave to soak overnight. Next day, boil the beans in fresh water in a saucepan for 10 minutes and drain well. Layer the bacon, onions and beans in the saucepan, season with pepper, add the bayleaf and then pour over sufficient water or stock to cover. Bring to the boil, cover the saucepan and simmer gently for 1½ to 2 hours or until the bacon and beans are tender. Remove the bayleaf and serve with boiled potatoes and cabbage or carrots. Serves 4 to 6.

Casserole of Beef with Chestnuts

Chestnuts give a deliciously nutty flavour to this simple beef casserole.

**15-20 chestnuts, roughly chopped
(tinned or fresh)
2 lb stewing steak, cubed
Seasoned flour
1 oz butter
1 large onion, sliced**

**4 tomatoes, peeled and
roughly chopped (optional)
½ pint beef stock, or ¼ pint stock
and ¼ pint red wine mixed
Salt and black pepper
Pinch of ground nutmeg**

Set oven to 325°F or Mark 3. If using fresh chestnuts split the skins with a knife and cook them in hot water for about 5 minutes; then, while still warm, remove the outer skins and the inner membranes. Toss the steak in the seasoned flour. Melt the butter in a frying pan and fry the onion until soft. Add the steak and brown lightly on all sides. Put the steak and onion into a casserole dish. Add the tomatoes, if desired, the stock or stock and red wine, seasoning and the nutmeg, then stir in the chestnuts. Cover and cook for 1½ to 2 hours or until the meat is tender. Serve with braised celery. Serves 4 to 6.

Sausage Stew

Thick, meaty pork sausages from a good butcher are best for this dish.
Try using spicy flavoured sausages for variety.

2 lbs pork sausages	**1 teaspoon mixed herbs**
2 tablespoons cooking oil	**1 teaspoon sugar**
1 medium onion, chopped	**1 dessertspoon cornflour**
2 cloves garlic, chopped	**Salt and pepper**
Large tin of tomatoes, roughly chopped	**¹/₂ pt vegetable stock**
1 tablespoon tomato purée	**2 cups frozen peas**

Cut the sausages in half. Heat 1 tablespoon of oil in a large saucepan and fry the sausages slowly, until browned. Remove and set aside. Add another tablespoon of oil to the pan and fry the onion and garlic until soft but not brown. Replace the sausages and add the chopped tomatoes, tomato purée, herbs and sugar and stir. Mix the cornflour with a tablespoon of stock in a bowl then stir in the remainder of the stock and mix well. Add to the saucepan, stir and season well. Bring to the boil, cover and simmer for 35 to 40 minutes, adding more boiling water if required during cooking. Add the peas 5 minutes before the end of the cooking time. Serves 4 to 6.

METRIC CONVERSIONS

The weights, measures and oven temperatures used in the preceding recipes can be easily converted to their metric equivalents. The conversions listed below are only approximate, having been rounded up or down as may be appropriate.

Weights

Avoirdupois	Metric
1 oz.	just under 30 grams
4 oz. (¼ lb.)	app. 115 grams
8 oz. (½ lb.)	app. 230 grams
1 lb.	454 grams

Liquid Measures

Imperial	Metric
1 tablespoon (liquid only)	20 millilitres
1 fl. oz.	app. 30 millilitres
1 gill (¼ pt.)	app. 145 millilitres
½ pt.	app. 285 millilitres
1 pt.	app. 570 millilitres
1 qt.	app. 1.140 litres

Oven Temperatures

	°Fahrenheit	Gas Mark	°Celsius
Slow	300	2	150
	325	3	170
Moderate	350	4	180
	375	5	190
	400	6	200
Hot	425	7	220
	450	8	230
	475	9	240

Flour as specified in these recipes refers to plain flour unless otherwise described.